How I Advanced my Artworl

By

Christopher Cairns

CW00894267

Table of Content

Watson and Holmes
Hold That Pose – one
Hold that Pose – two
Hold That Pose
Abreast – basics
Abreast – stage 2
Abreast – Finished
Ballerina – stage one
Ballerina – stage two
Ballerina with dark background
Ballerina – finished
A **Look of an Artist – Basic**
A **Look of an Artist – stage two**
A **Look of an Artist**
Paul Newman – stage one
Robert Redford – stage one
Paul Newman – stage two
Robert – stage two
The Cowboys – Butch and Sundance
Anne – stage one
Anne – stage two
Anne
Mary
Incomplete One
Incomplete Two
Hardy
Maira
Incomplete Three
Yusuf – Early stage of completion
Yusuf
Drawing inside the lines – First in a series – nude one
Life Drawing – Nude Two – Drawing inside the lines
Bronte – stage one
Bronte – Finished
Taking a bath
Muse
Muse Two

Introduction

Having had success with my first book 'My Artistic Journey using Pointillism' I decided to continue that journey with this book 'How I advanced my artwork using Pointillism'
What do I mean by 'How'?

Its one thing to see a completed piece of artwork, but what budding artists want to know; how did the artist reach that stage of completion. Where did he begin? What was he thinking along the way as his artwork began to take shape? This publication will hopefully answer those questions as I will show the different stages of each piece and add comments to show you my thoughts.

As with my original book, I will continue in the same vein by listing all my artwork whether good or bad. I will also add a note to the piece together with what I liked about the work and what I don't like. As artists, we never complete a piece of art perfectly to our liking. Usually we make mistakes; sometimes it's a line in the wrong place or a limb not quite in position or maybe we've added too much shading. I will be honest in my appraisal so you'll see from my notes exactly how I feel about my own artwork.

I hope you enjoy watching my progress and advancement with Pointillism and that by the end you'll have a better idea of what not to do when beginning your journey into Pointillism.

Red White and Blue

Completed August 2017 on A2 Cartridge paper

Red white and Blue

I've previously explained the beauty that can be seen in the human form and from an artistic point of view especially for a man; the female body is something pleasurable to look at. Having received positive comments for my past drawings of the female form, I decided to continue along that same vein.

What do I like about this piece?

I'm happy with it. It has all the elements a portrait should have; the composition is good with the added colour for the brassiere and knickers. The subject is positioned nicely central to the paper and fills the space to an acceptable level. But most of all, it's pleasing to the eye.

The cleavage with its darker shading immediately draws the viewer's attention to the full bust held in with the red lace cups. The added colour from the underwear becoming the secondary focal point because of the less striking colour of the blue and white but nonetheless completes its purpose; hence the title Red White and Blue.

What I don't like.

Looking at the artwork now that it's finished, I'm not overly happy with the head. Having the top of the ladies head missing just below the eyes is a definite no no. one of the key features with portraits is the connection the portrait has with the onlooker. When including a face; the onlooker would naturally stare into the eyes of the subject to make that connection. Not including the eyes in this portrait has definitely taken away some of its appeal, I think.

A Close Up

As you can see from the close up, I've stuck with the two different size marker pens. The thicker marker pen was used to highlight the darker shading, while the thinner marker pen with its finer knib was used to emphasise the tonal shading, and to give depth and contour.

One of the problems I had to contend with was the use of the two **colour** pens. I only had the use of a thin pen at the time, so this caused some concern because I was unable to create darker shading. I was not overly concerned at the time, but looking back, I can see how a darker red or blue would have really emphasised the material giving more depth and texture.

I'll need to think about obtaining the correct tools before I begin my next project.

ISLA

Completed September 2017 on A2 cartridge paper

Isla

I draw this portrait because Isla is the daughter of a friend of mine. Bringing the face of your subject close really gives you an opportunity to build on the personality of that person. The innocence and beauty portrayed in a young child can be most appealing. Usually you would position your subject so that seventy percent of the drawing area would be your subject while thirty percent would fill the background. You will notice that in this instance, I brought my subject really close and filled the whole space; is that wrong? No. the two key features within this portrait are the face and hand. Having included those within the frame and having the darker shading down the right side and the pale shading for the girls dress below; really presents this piece off well.

What I like about this piece?

The portrait has a nice feel. The composition is well balanced with the right amount of shading on the left and right side with the subject central and filling the space adequately.

The reflective light centrally focussed on the smiling face really brings the image to life allowing the onlooker to take in the smiling eyes and lips of a young girl happy to be holding a flower.

What I don't like.

I purposely left a lot of detail out of the bulk of hair because I wanted the focus to be on the child's face and not on the exterior details. Maybe my decision was wrong but at this time I feel that I did make the right decision. I'll let you decide.

Black and White

I really wanted to draw a full colour portrait. Having reached this stage using only black dots I've come to a crossroads. Do I continue and finish another black and white portrait or do I continue on with my initial plan and add colour.

As an artist, I'm sure we've all felt this way. You look at your piece of art and think; should I carry on, or is it finished? If I carry on and add to the picture I could end up doing something I'd regret and possibly ruin it. What should I do? You ask yourself.
Even if you ask someone else and they say.
"That's perfect! Do not do anything else to it, its wonderful"

Deep in your heart, you know you want to make it better and you've probably spent a long time on it already so following those words of wisdom from a friend may be the right course to take. But will you regret it later on, maybe you'll be mulling it over for the rest of the day thinking, I should continue.

I find myself in this very predicament, I wanted to add colour to my next piece of art and here I am just looking at it thinking I may ruin what I've achieved.

What to do?

I did say I was going to use colour in my next piece of art so I should stick to my guns and do it. If I ruin it, at least I'll have tried.

RIGHT, LET'S ADD COLOUR!

(Note: for those looking at these portraits using a kindle, you may only see black and white. Full colour portraits completed in this book can be seen on saatchiart.com/dragstar61)

That Look

Completed September 2017 on A2 cartridge paper

That look

"Wow. I love it;" Came the reply from my wife.
"What a relief" I say to myself.
This piece of art was particularly challenging in that I'd never used a variety of colours to create tones and skin colour before in pointillism. Over the past year having just focussed on black and white dots to create shade, contrast, tones and composition; I'd noticed that my 'Artistic eye' has changed focus somewhat.

What do I think of this piece?

I must admit that I was unsure about the whole process while I was building up the piece of art. It definitely was a learning curve and I'm pleased with the end result.

What I don't like.

Maybe I should have added more detail to the hair and I'm not sure about the colour of the hand. Because of the lighting and the position of the hand, it should be a different colour to the lower back; which it is, so maybe I have got it right, I don't know, I think I'll let you decide.

Shanaz

Completed early October 2017 on A2 cartridge paper

<u>Shanaz</u>

A work colleague asked me to draw a picture of his wife.
Ok
I want it to be a surprise so she doesn't know.
No problem, I just need a picture to work from.
Then Yusuf presented me with this photograph

What do I like about this piece?

So what can I say about this picture. Where do I start?
The positives, I've finished it.

What I don't like.

No honestly, this was a hard piece to complete. So where did I go
wrong? For me, it's all about the preparation and planning. If I'd
taken my time in laying out the image correctly before filling in, I'm
sure that would have resolved some of the negative aspects of the
piece. I immediately started off with a thicker marker pen which
inhibited my ability for accuracy, particularly around the facial
features. One of the problems is in the composition. The lady in
question is pouting her lips; this gives a distorted view of her face
and so trying to portray her facial expressions correctly with thicker
knibs is definitely difficult. Had I thought about the subject before
starting, I would have maybe zoomed in on her face and omitted the
rest of her body so more detail could be added. By using more of the
paper would have reduced the impact of larger knibs and therefore
provided me with greater freedom; if you know what I mean.

So really the moral of this tale; think about your subject and how you
want to present it before ever putting pen to paper or paint to canvas.
This will save a lot of negative thoughts and anxiety especially when
you've put in hours and hours into a piece, knowing it's all going
downhill.

Mika

Completed early October 2017 on A2 cartridge paper

Mika

Having had a disaster with the portrait of Shanaz, I really need to build myself up again by having a success. This made me think of returning to a previous style and a simple portrait and a return to using black and white.

What I like about this piece?

I like the simplicity of it all. The stark contrast between light and dark is so appealing. The overall composition is good with the darker edges drawing the onlooker's eyes to the beauty of the female with her lovely smile. I didn't want to over complicate this piece so there's a lot of detail missing that could have been included.

From a distance the piece looks quite angelic and complete. It gives you the sense of happiness and maybe a desire to find out what the female is thinking. I left the bottom right corner blank to allow the viewer the freedom to draw their own conclusions as to what the lady is looking at. Whatever it is, it's something she's pleased with.

I wanted the overall piece to lift up the onlooker's spirits and as I examine the piece now that it's finished, I think I've achieved what I set out to do.

What I don't like

Maybe I could have included the lady's shoulders to present the portrait a little more in a traditional style. Other than that, I think I wouldn't change a thing.

Seduction- filling in the background

A picture of me hard at work adding dots to my next piece of artwork.

This can be a very time consuming process, as you can see from the image, the A2 paper covers quite an area while the small knib on a marker pen is very small in contrast.

I wanted you to see the comparison so when I explain how long it took me to fill in the background on a piece of art, you'll understand just what I mean. Bye the way this image only shows the top right hand corner of the full piece as you will see in my next completed image.

Just for your information and understanding, the image shown before shows approximately four to five hours work. I hope to complete the artwork tomorrow after a further three hours maybe. May I also remind you that when I say five hours, I mean five hours applying constant dots to the paper; that is dot, dot, dot every second; or in clear English, I press the knib of my marker pen onto the paper three times every second for one thousand eight hundred seconds which equates to a staggering fifty four thousand dots.

That's what I've completed so far, and I still have thirty two thousand four hundred dots to go. These figures may not be completely accurate but they sure feel that way. Maybe one day I will count them, just so I can specifically say for sure how many dots are on the paper. We'll see.

Seduction

Completed mid October 2017 on A2 cartridge paper

Seduction

What motivated me to draw this piece? I wanted to create a story within the picture. What is she thinking? Why is she in the dark and is she wearing clothes? Maybe she is wearing a strapless dress but cold. Maybe she's worried about the person looking at her. Is she nervous having removed her own clothes and now awaits her prospective lover to remove his?

Creating a piece of art that poses many questions can be most intriguing and interesting to the onlooker. It can mean different things to different people and so it becomes a most sort after piece of artwork.

What do I like about this piece?

I think the composition is nice and again well balanced. The subject is central and with the darker areas on both sides and both lower corners, really keeps the onlookers view centralised within the piece. The overall detail is good from the flowing hair and hands and the tonal shading to an acceptable level. Overall I'm quite pleased with this piece.

What I don't like.

I could have made the subject a little darker and more tone to the flesh. Maybe a little more detail to the hair? And possibly adding a light reflection in her left eye, maybe would improve the overall piece.

Initial outline

I thought you may like to see the piece of artwork I'm currently working on. Instead of just showing you the finished artwork, I've decided to show you each stage so you'll get a better understanding of how I create each piece.

To begin with, as you can tell from the initial drawing; I like to sketch the subject before hand to get all the proportions right as well as hopefully getting an idea of the composition. At this early stage, it's much easier to make the necessary adjustments while I'm still using pencil. Once you start to apply ink to the paper; there's no turning back and any wrong application of ink, could result in disaster.

As you can see from the drawing, there's not a lot of detail involved. You just want to get the outlines and positioning correct before you start to fill in.

So, let's move onto the filling in part.

Stage two – Admired from afar

Applying darker shading

At this stage, I like to begin with the darker areas just to set the subject firmly within the piece. I usually begin with the eyes, nose and mouth and then other darker areas so the whole composition can be seen clearly.

You may have noticed that I've basically just filled in the dress with dark black dots. There's no detail or tone at this stage, because I just want to fill in that space to give myself an overall picture of how the piece will look like.

Sometimes you can get carried away with constantly pressing dots onto the piece that you forget what you're doing. In this way, we're keeping it basic so if I need to go back later and make adjustments, I could.

Remember at each stage to step back away from the piece and look at your work. Things always look different when you look from a better vantage point and standing six feet away can give you a clearer view of the overall piece.

Let's move on to stage three.

Stage Three – Admired from Afar

A little more detail

Here I've added more detail using a finer marker pen with shading around the face and cheekbones as well as shading on the chest and shoulders. You don't need a lot of shading but enough for you to see the contours as you step back to get your better view.

I've also added highlights to the hair so I know what part of the hair not to fill in when I begin using the thicker darker marker.

You may also have noticed that I've still not added finer detail as yet. That will be added once I've got the overall piece in place. So what to do next?

The Hair!

Completed the Darker area's

Building up a picture can take quite a while as you can see. Filling in the darker areas can aide the process of getting a clearer picture as to the finished article. You never completely fill in a section as a house builder wouldn't completely finish one wall of a house before starting on the second wall. Foundations have to be laid and then each layer upon layer needs to be added to finally finishing the last layer when you eventually see the full structure.

That's still not to say the final structure is the completed article. If you darken one area, this will have an impact on other areas. Remember you need the overall piece to be balanced, so darkening one side will result in you having to darken the other side to keep the overall picture the same.

Now that I have the full structure in place, I still need to fill in the details as you would put furniture into a house to make it a home.

I need to fill in the darker area's more and maybe a little more shading around the face.

Stage Five – Admired from Afar

The darker dress really emphasises the rest of her. So maybe I'll add more shading to the hair to give depth.

Admired from Afar

Completed 19 October 2017 on A2 cartridge paper

Admired from afar

Finished I think. I get that same feeling with every piece of artwork; is it finished? I don't know, maybe I'll just add a little here or there. The problem is, were never really happy with what we've achieved and so we will always think, we need to do something more.

Looking at the piece now that I'm finished, I can see there's area's I could improve, maybe darken the back of the hand or maybe darken the lips to bring the onlookers focus to her mouth. To be honest, I'm quite pleased with the piece as it is, so maybe I'll just leave it and move on to my next project.

As you can see from stage five, I'd filled in more detail with the hand and darkened the areas around the cleavage and under the chin as well as the light areas at the back of the neck so as a whole, I think it look's complete.

What I like about this piece?

The composition is good and the detail is acceptable; bearing in mind that with pointillism, the idea is that you don't put too much detail onto the piece because you're working with dots. By stepping away and viewing the artwork from a distance will tell you if the piece is finished or not. Let me step back for a moment and look.

Yes, it's finished.

What I don't like.

This is a difficult one as I'm pretty well pleased with the overall result. If I had to find something I would change; maybe I could add more detail around the bust line and possibly darkened the ladies lips.

Clint Eastwood Stage 1

As mentioned before, I like to get some of the darker areas down so you can get a feel of the artwork. Drawing a cowboy wearing a Stetson really takes up a larger section of the artwork in shadow. This can prove to be beneficial in that the piece takes on shape fairly quickly. So I concentrate on the outlines as well as the eyes and any other darker sections which can be seen in the coat and neck tie.

Clint Eastwood Stage 2

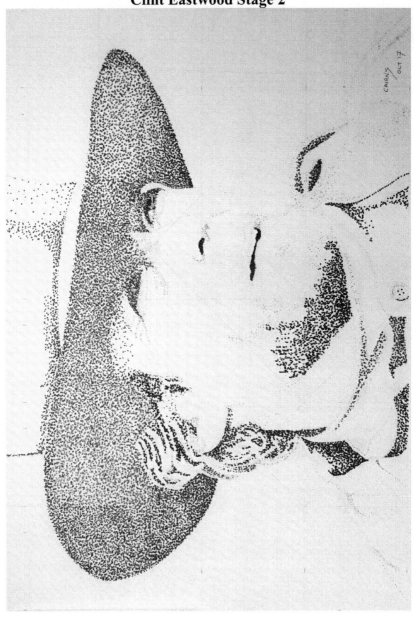

As you can see, the piece really starts to look good from the larger dark areas from under his hat to the shading from the folds in his clothing.

Looking good so far, let's add more shading.

Clint Eastwood Stage 3

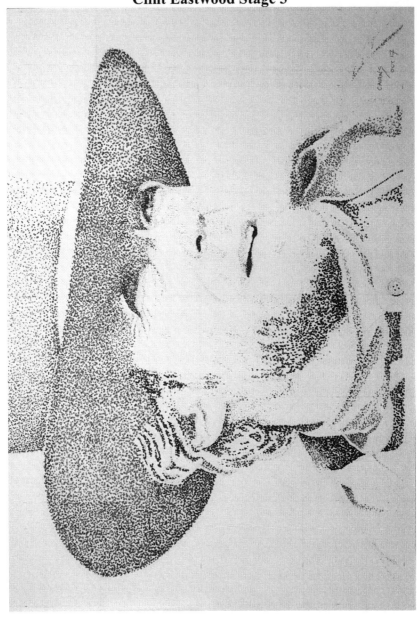

At this stage, I've added quite a bit of finer detail, showing the shadows and contours around his face. The filling in on the hat is more complete but still has quite a way to go and the detail from the clothing has taken on much more shape.

I think I'll start adding darker shading now to the underside of the hat to get a contrast. The top of his hat still needs darker shadows on the left side while the light reflecting off the right side of the hat, needs to be clearer.

Clint Eastwood

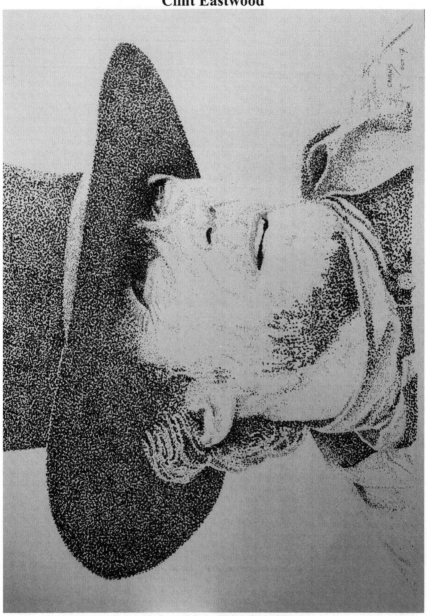

Completed late October 2017

Clint Eastwood

As always, I reached a point where I decided enough's enough. I completed the shading and subtle tones from light to dark from the right side of his hat to the left side. A little more filling in on the shading on the coat lapels and the hair and thought, yes, I don't think I need to do anymore.

What I like about this piece?

Standing back and looking at this piece, I quite like it. The composition is good and the subject is nicely balanced. The dark Stetson contrasting with the dark shadows around his neck tie really presents the portrait off well. I like the detail show his rugged handsome looks.

What I don't like.

If I was to be over critical, I would have to say I'm not totally pleased with his right eye. I know the brim of his hat casts a shadow across his face but I still feel his right eye is too dark. Maybe I'm wrong. Overall I love it.

That Smile

Completed end October 2017 on A2 cartridge paper

<u>That Smile</u>

At this juncture I wanted to add a portrait that would make you feel good. A beautiful smiling woman sounds about right and so 'That Smile' was created.
I'm really pleased with this piece. From an initial observation the artwork looks delightful, joyful, happy and fresh. There are so many adjectives I could use to describe this piece, needless to say, it makes me smile.

What I like about this piece?

There's a nice balance with this piece, the darker shading compliments the light tones making its composition complete. The large smile just above centre really draws your attention while the light colour hair, robe and low cut nightie finishes off the piece without stealing your focus.

The darker shading on the left side showing the fall of her dressing gown, the dark rim of her nightie and the outline of her hair alongside the shadow of her hair falling across her left arm on the right side of this piece is perfectly balanced. It becomes a perfect example of how to create a simple piece of art which is light, yet striking at the same time.

What I don't like.

If I was to be critical I would have to say maybe the shading on the right side of her face and right arm is too dark? I'm not sure. It's difficult to find fault when something brings you joy. I hope it brings you joy too.

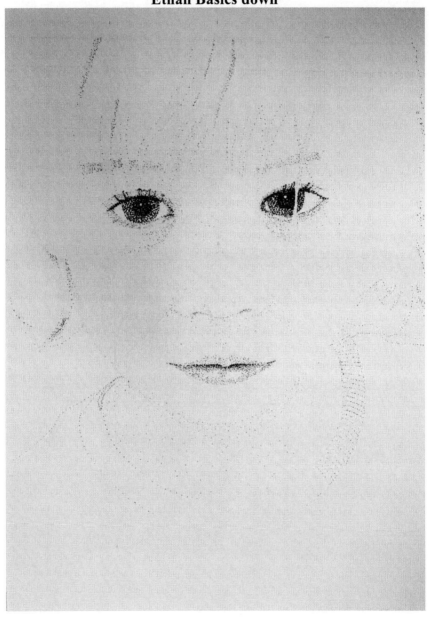

Having already completed a portrait of two of my Granddaughters my wife pestered me into doing a portrait of my Grandson; what could I say. OK.

My wife presented me with a photograph she took of my Grandson Ethan a few years ago.
'I love this one' she exclaimed.
Looking all gooey eyed. I took a look at the picture and thought, it's really bright. The light almost obliterates the details around the face and with Ethan having bright blonde hair; you can't see his hair at all.

I do like the photograph and as my wife wanted this portrait done, I thought, I may as well give it a try.

The key focus on successfully completing this task would have to be the darker areas. With so much light, the darker shades would bring this piece of artwork to life. As with all my pieces, I usually begin with putting down the darker sections to bring the portrait together, and so the eyes were a key feature I had to get right.

I made sure the position of the eyes fell central to the artwork as these were to represent the main focus from onlookers.

Ethan

Completed end of October 2017

Ethan

What can I say about the completed portrait?

I quite like the simplicity of the piece; it captures the innocence of Ethan at this age. The bright eyes looking intently at the camera, wondering what the small little box is for that his Grand Mother is holding.

What I like about this piece?

The composition is nicely set out with the overall feel of the subject being balanced in the piece. The darker shading on either side with the darker sections highlighting the hair; all compliments each other.

What I don't like.

I did say the perfect proportions for a portrait, is a seventy, thirty split. Seventy percent being the subject while thirty percent the background. I feel that the subject takes up too much of the overall piece leaving me to think, it's too overcrowded. Maybe the subject should have been a little further back to get the whole of the head into the frame.

Maybe I should have put my foot down and told my wife that the photograph wasn't suitable, running the risk of not being fed. Maybe not! I'm hungry and my wife likes the piece anyway.

Enjoying the Beach

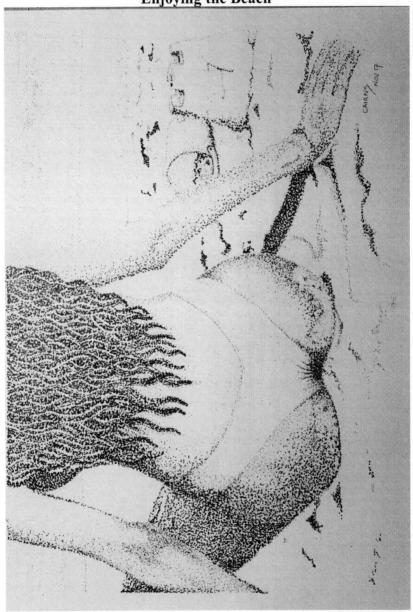

Completed November 2017 on A2 cartridge paper

<u>Enjoying the beach</u>

I thought I would try something different this time and create a scene. For most of us, we've experienced this sight in front of us on many a beach. A beautiful woman sat with the trace of sand stuck to her backside. You try to enjoy the views of the gentle tide lapping against the shore and maybe you spot a seagull high up in the sky. The warm sun on your skin warms you through and you breathe in the salty sea breeze, and then your eyes return to the woman sat in front of you. This image can conjure up so many thoughts into your head. Maybe I should have said; questions into your head. Why is this beautiful woman alone? I wonder how old, she is? I wonder if she works out? Is she single? I'm in love.

What I like about this piece?

I like it, its simple, not overly crowded and the scene tells a story. Maybe a different story to different people but in any case, each individual looking at this piece will ask a question.

Why is there a sand castle next to her?
Does she have a child?
Where are all the other people?

I'll let you make your own minds up as to what questions you would like to ask. For me, I'm happy.

What I don't like.

Maybe the hair is too regulated, maybe I should have drawn her hair slightly ruffled or windswept or maybe wet from having been in the sea. Maybe also I should have centred the subject on the page to produce a more balanced composition.

Basic outline drawn.

Following the same procedure as with all my pieces of artwork; I've laid out the groundwork and positioned the subject on the paper in the right proportions. Following the initial pencil outline, I've added fine dots to confirm my proportions ready for filling in.

Behind the Curtains – stage two

Notice that I've filled in more of the darker areas to get a sense of the overall picture.

I initially wanted to draw a naked female from the waist up but then changed my mind and positioned my subject behind a set of curtains.

The idea came to me after recalling the occasion when I saw a similar scene many years ago. I suppose the lady in question didn't expect someone to be walking along the pavement early in the morning, but then again; who looks out of their window completely naked?

In any case, I thought it would portray an interesting piece. So onto completing this artwork, what to do next? More detail, I think.

Behind the Curtains

Completed 4th November 2017 on A2 cartridge paper

Behind the curtains

Having had a change in thought after I began drawing this portrait, I think it's worked out quite nicely. The subject is nicely placed and central, which is always a good idea. The dark hair and dark shadows hiding part of her face really brings your focus straight to that look.

The detail on the upper body is good showing shadow and tone allowing the onlooker to get a sense of shape. The darker right side of the piece highlights the part of her body that remains in shadow with the left side illuminated from the light outside shows off the contours of her athletic body.

I didn't want the curtains to distract the viewer from the more important feature of the artwork being the lady, so I kept the curtains pale in colour. The light inside the room again keeps the overall feel of the piece bright.

What I like about this piece?

I particularly like the detail around the chest and shoulders using the thinner marker pen alongside the thicker marker pen. You can definitely get the sense of shape and shadow.

What I don't like.

I think the eyes makeup around her right eye is too dark and although her left eye is obscured by her hair, I think I should have added more detail to the shape of her left eye.

Profile – stage one

Basics down

I know this portrait is going to be a challenge because I'm drawing a woman from the side. Why is that a challenge? Because a large section of the portrait on the left side will consist mainly of her hair, which will unbalance the piece of art.

Having laid down the basics, I decided to fill in briefly the darker areas to get an overall shape of the finished portrait.

Profile – stage two

At this point I'm a little concerned about the amount of dark hair the girl has. Usually it wouldn't matter if someone has a lot of hair, but in this instance, because she is looking to the right, the mass of dark hair takes up a quarter of the image leaving the portrait a little lob sided.

My intention was to give the lady jet black hair to create a kind of sultry look with her dark eye makeup and pouting lips, but now that I've got this far, I can see the large black mass could work against me.

The problem I've got is I'm working with ink, so I can't rub it out or cover it over. So what to do? I like the image as it is with her looking over to the right, not that I could change that even if I wanted to, so how am I going to recover from what may be a disaster.

Let me think.

Profile – stage three

Recovered I think.

I don't know if you've ever experienced that sinking feeling. Not the experience of going down in a boat, but one where you feel that no matter what you do, you're doomed to failure.

I had that very thought before completing stage three. I don't know about you, but I feel as though I recovered quite well considering the predicament I left myself in. The horrible thought of filling in a large mass of hair and ruining the artwork gave me that sick feeling in my stomach. Not that I loved this piece so much, no, it's the fact that I would have lost all those hours already spent on this artwork.

OK so I'm on a high again. So what to do next? I need to fill in more shading around the hand and shoulders, arm and bust.

Profile

Completed 5 November 2017 on A2 cartridge paper

Profile

Well I have to say, this had me worried for a while, but in the end, I'm pleased with the finished results.

What I like about this piece?

It's simplicity I think.

The dark mass of hair could have been a problem but applying pointillism in lines to show the contour and flow of the hair, really works. The natural gaps between the hair strands, lends to breaking up the dark mass, providing shape. The large dark area mainly focussed towards the top of the piece forces the onlooker to look down towards the lighter areas of the beautiful woman seductive stare.

The subject is nicely presented covering most of the area. She's central and although the dark hair runs down from top to lower left, the piece feels right because the remainder of the area is light.

It's not your typical portrait, but it feels right.

What I don't like.

I've drawn the lady's left arm coming up between her breasts, is that right? Maybe her arm should have been behind both breasts. Does it matter? I don't know, I suppose it all depends on how she's standing; is she standing straight or is she twisted slightly. I'll leave it up to you to decide.

Relax – stage one

We've all experienced the sight of a beautiful woman relaxing in the chair enjoying the sun. Maybe it's hot and she's taken her top off revealing her brassiere. She doesn't mind because you're not overlooked and she just wants to enjoy the beautiful day

This scenario gave me the inspiration to draw this next piece. Now that I've laid down the basics, what do I do next? I like the composition and I think it'll work in black and white as I want the contrast between the bright Noon Day Sun to radiate off her naked skin. This would create a striking contrast, I think.

Then, I do the opposite and pick up a colour pen.

Relax – stage two

What have I done! I exclaim.
I don't know why I chose to add colour, but now that I have, I'd better continue.

Standing back, I look and think. 'I don't know where I want to go with this.'
I think the only thing to do is continue and maybe hope for the best.

Right! Let's fill in the hair to get some shape.

Relax – stage three

OK, it's looking better.
I like the hair and the contrasting green brassiere really divides your focus.

I'm happy with it so far, just need to fill in the background a little and finish off with the shading to emphasise the contours and tones of the skin.

Relax

Completed 9th November 2017 on A2 cartridge paper

Relax

I finally reached the point where I think I've finished. Having filled
in the back of the chair and added extra shading to emphasise her
muscle definition and feminine shape, I think the portrait is
complete.

What I like about this piece?

I like the addition of colour, it's not how I originally wanted the
piece to look like but all in all, I'm pretty happy with the results.

What I don't like.

Looking back at this piece the mistakes come flooding to mind. For
one, the composition is wrong. The lady's head runs off the top of
the page. There should be more colour added to her flesh tones.
There are too much light areas across her skin. Not enough shading
under her chin. Could I go on? Yes but I wont. Not one of my best
and there's too much wrong with this piece to change and make
good, so I'll move on to my next piece.

Sherlock Holmes – basic

This is part of my Holmes and Watson piece. Having completed the outline, I've pressed on and filled in some of the darker shading. Initially, I was a little worried with this because I find Robert Downey JR has a difficult face to draw. Every portrait I've seen of Robert has always been 80 percent accurate which doesn't bode well for future artists wishing to capture his facial features correctly.

Now that I've shaded in some of the face, I can see that it's coming together nicely.

I just wanted to mention that the portrait has Jude Law on the left and Robert Downey JR on the right. I'd already completed the basics for Jude Law's character by this point, so I've been a little nervous about getting Sherlock's face just right. It's always difficult drawing two characters, worrying that you'll do a perfect job on the first and ruin the second, and so spoil the whole piece.

Looking at my progress, I'm comfortably happy with the results so far. Lets hope I don't mess up later; I'll let you be the judge of that.

Anyway, here's the basic portrait I've already completed of Dr John Watson.

Dr John Watson – Basics

I found this to be a little easier than Robert Downey Jr for the simple fact that Jude Law has a more distinctive face.
How do I feel about what I'd achieved so far?

I like it, the eyes look ok and once I've filled in more of the darker sections, I think it will all come together.

Not that I'm making excuses or anything, but, remember earlier on the importance of planning a piece out before ever putting pen to paper. I did plan this one but I also made a mistake in the positioning.

I'd planned for the two main characters to be looking at each other with a gap in the middle and similar spacing either side of each character. I think I did the measuring early in the morning and not yet woken up. Well that's my excuse. Anyway, you may have noticed the back of Dr Watson's hat is chopped off   (oops) sorry. Maybe those who admire the finished piece might not notice. Let's keep this between you and me shall we.

Just need to finish it now and upload the finished piece for you to see what I mean. Fingers crossed.

Watson and Holmes

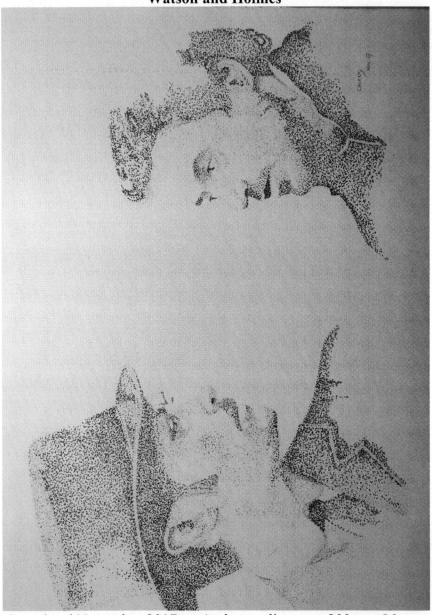

Completed November 2017 on Archers velin paper 200gsm 56cm x 76cm

Watson and Holmes

Finished my latest portrait of Jude Law and Robert Downey Jr portrayed as Dr Watson and Sherlock Holmes.

Looking at the portraits of the two subjects, they're nicely placed (although Watson is just slightly too far left for a well composed portrait, as previously mentioned.) The subject's heads relate their relative heights and so presenting the subjects accurately. The eyes are fixed on each other which bind the two separate characters together making it, one piece of artwork.

You may have wondered why I left the subject matter incomplete. To be honest, I thought it would add to the desirability of owning such a piece. Remember, not every piece of artwork has to be complete. Leaving something out can be most desirable in the eyes of a prospective buyer. It can lead the onlooker to wonder why something is missing, why did the artist leave that out? It would have been easy enough to fill in that little bit, so why is it missing?

Looking at the piece now that it's finished, I'm glad I left part of it incomplete.

What I like about this piece?

The composition is nice, it lends to the story as they both face each other in conversation. There's a nice balance with light and shade with the use of a thicker marker pen for the dark shadows and thin marker pen for the subtle tonal changes.

What I don't like.

Maybe I should have added more detail from shoulder level to link these two characters together as having the plain background and the plain gap between them makes the characters seem separated.

Hold That Pose – one

We often see beautiful women in perfect poses with perfect makeup and hair. That was my inspiration for this next piece. How many photographs are taken while the model holds that pose, perfectly still. As before, I've drawn the basics using pencil, getting the positioning right and dimensions all in proportion before putting ink onto paper.

This time highlighting the facial features, bust and arms were key to getting a rounded out overview of the subject. Next it's onto filling in more detail with the bolder marker pen.

It certainly makes a difference once you fill in the hair. And in this case you can see that the picture really comes together. So onto more shading I think to really bring the contours of the body to the fore.

Hold That Pose

Completed 15 November 2017 on Archers Velin paper 200gsm
56cm x 76cm

Hold that pose

I like this piece of artwork; it's simple but holds all the key features for a good portrait. The subject is central to the paper and the composition is well balance with the dark hair capping the subject at the top, with the long lengths of dark hair falling nicely down the right side, drawing you into the picture.

There can always be a danger in over emphasising the shading of the extremities, which can draw the onlooker's focus away from what is pivotal to the piece; in this case the face. With this piece of artwork, you know the shoulders, bust and arms are there, but they don't compete as a focal point.

What I like about this piece?

I like the overall composition. I like the hair with the darker shadows emphasising the locks of hair folding over each other.

What I don't like.

Maybe I could have added a little more detail to the arm and shoulders to show shape and tone.

Abreast – basics

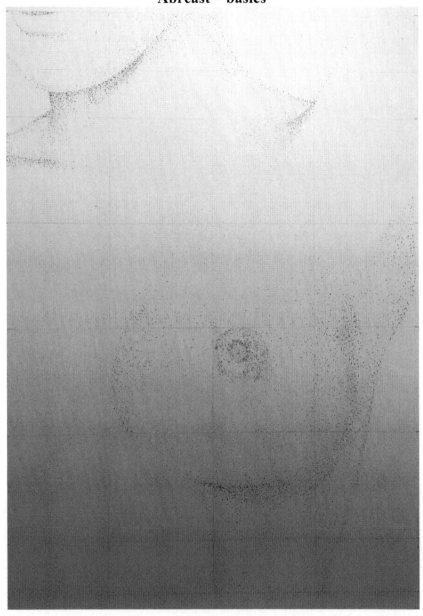

There's always a fascination for men with women's breasts.
Maybe it's just because we don't have any shapely breasts ourselves I don't know.
I thought it would be good practice to carry on drawing parts of the anatomy, and so I've included, not breasts but a breast.

As you can see, I've laid down the basics. This time I wanted to concentrate on just using a fine knib marker pen because with skin tones, it's probably better to use a fine knib so you can highlight the imperfections of the skin more easily. This process of adding one dimensional marks onto a paper creates unity in that there aren't bolder sections causing your eyes to focus on. Rather, the unified dots create a natural flow in the subject, making it easier to see tone and contour.

Now the basics are down. I think I'll move on to adding more shading in the hope of getting a clearer view of body and shape. Here goes.

Abreast – stage 2

It's slowly taking shape and I mean slowly. Having a large area to fill and using solely the fine marker pen is proving to be very time consuming. As you can see, I've added darker shading under the chin and across the shoulder to show more shape to my portrait. I've built up a larger section just to the right of her left breast to help build up tone and contour. Still plenty to do so I'll get right too it and add more shading.

Abreast – Finished

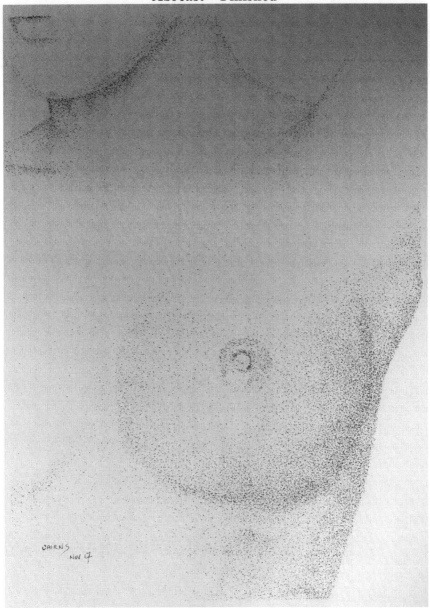

Completed 18 November 2017 on A2 cartridge paper

<u>Abreast</u>

This was an interesting piece of art to create. As mentioned earlier, I wanted to create this using only a fine knib pen so I could unify the portrait bringing a natural flow of tone, contour and balance. There's always a difficulty in using one sized knib to create depth of shading in that the thousand pointillism dots concentrated in one area, has to be replicated in other areas of the subject to balance the piece out.

For example; I applied a natural shadow under the breast to show where the breast attached to the ribcage. Once I darkened the shadow to the underside of the breast to show the contour of the underside of the breast, I lost definition to where the breast was now attached.

Increasing shade in one area forced me to add more shade to another area to keep the piece balance and this became a juggling act in that, if I wanted to add contrast, I lost contour and depth. I must say this was a challenging project.

What I like about this piece?

I like the simplicity of it all. The darker shadow under the right side of the breast and the chin in the opposite corner; creates a natural top and bottom to this piece.

The use of a single sized knib, brings continuity and flow to the subject. There are no strong areas to steal your focus, so you're left with the two main areas to gaze at. The perfectly formed breast positioned just below centre, and the chin, neck and shoulders towards the top.

What I don't like.

Maybe I should have add a little more detail to the face and possibly added locks of hair to build up that secondary focal area.

Ballerina – stage one

I have drawn a ballerina before but as I wasn't too enamoured with it, I feel it's time to try and recreate something beautiful. The first thing I wanted to change was the positioning. The last ballerina was a full length drawing and didn't fill the paper fully, so this time, I thought about bringing her closer so I could increase the details.

So now I've positioned her correctly and got the basics drawn, let's concentrate on the details for stage two.

Ballerina – stage two

At this point I thought I had finished the artwork. I looked at it again and thought. "Do I need to do anything else?"

I don't know. So I got a second opinion from my wife.

"Anne, what do you think, do I need to do anything else like adding a dark background?" all the while hoping she would say. "No. that's perfect as it is."
Filling in the background would take forever so secretly I didn't want to do it. Then Anne replies. "I think you should fill in the background."

Ballerina with dark background

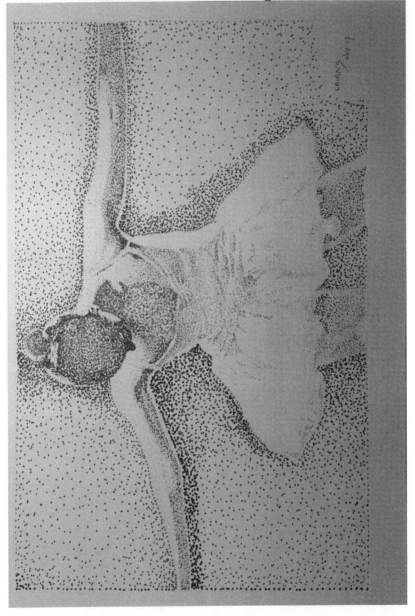

Ok, so it's looking better already. Just go so much filling in to do, it's going to take forever. I'll return with the finished piece when I'm finished. Maybe sometime tomorrow, I hope.

Ballerina – finished

Completed 19 November 2017 on A2 cartridge paper

Ballerina

Phew, finished at last. I thought it would take forever to fill in the background and my arm aches now. Was it worth it? I think so.

Adding the dark background really brings the ballerina to life, showing of all her reflective skin surfaces and her white tutu. In this instance the contrast is quite stunning as the ballerina holds her pose, poised to move on in her performance while the bright spotlight streams down from above.

What I like about this piece?

I love it. I like the composition. Her body takes up just the right amount of paper to demand your focus. The dark shadows on her head arms and legs; contrasting with the subtle folds of her tutu against the dark background really unites this piece of art.

What I don't like.

Sorry at this moment I can't think of anything I don't like.

A **Look of an Artist** – **Basic**

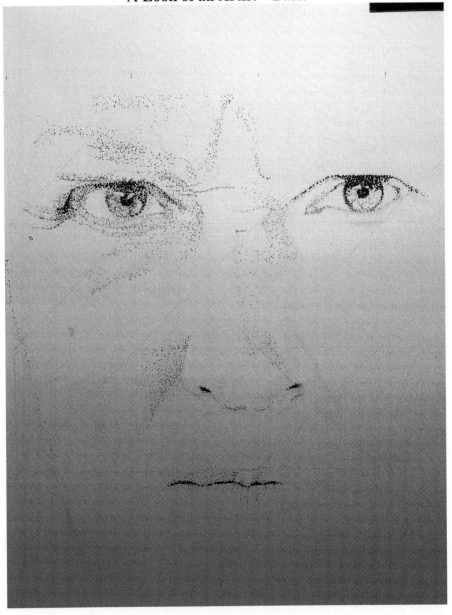

The look of an Artist came to mind having seen many self portraits presented as head and shoulder portraits or full portraits of the artist sat down with their head turned slightly towards the camera. I was more interested in getting a real close up; to be able to see right into the eyes and deep into the soul.

This initial drawing beginning with a few pencil lines followed by a fine marker pen to get the proportions right. It all looks good at this moment in time, so on to filling in more detail.

A **Look of an Artist – stage two**

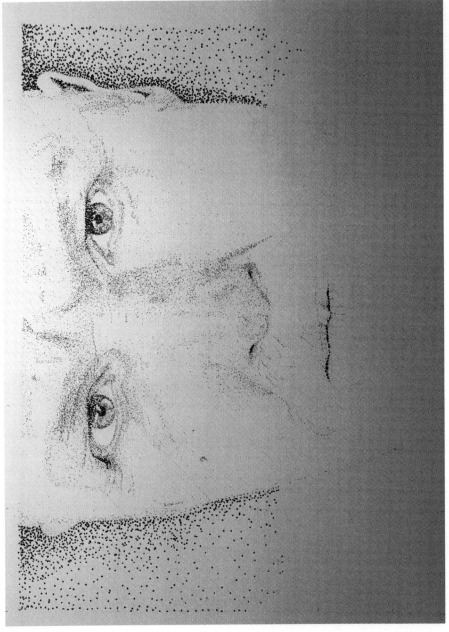

As before mentioned, I like to incorporate some darker shading early to really pull the piece together and to get a sense of how it will look when completed. Just by adding the darker shading on the sides with the odd touches for the eyes, nose and mouth helps the piece take shape. It's a nice technique to use before you spend hours and hours on a piece and not really know if the finished piece will turn out alright.

This way you've created some darker shading within a short space of time to get a sense of the completed piece and it also provides an opportunity to see if you need to make any adjustments in anyway before you've over committed yourself.

Looking at it now, I can see that it's all come together nicely. Just need to fill in around the mouth to get a complete picture before filling in more fully.

A **Look of an Artist**

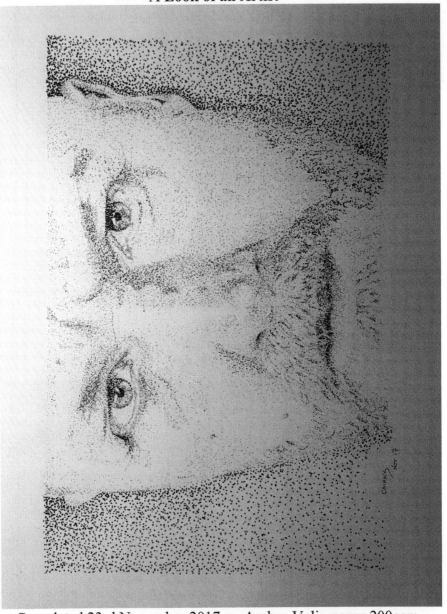

Completed 23rd November 2017 on Arches Velin paper 200gsm
56cm x 76cm

A Look of an Artist

In this piece I wanted to bring the subjects face closer so I could really highlight the imperfections and nuances of the man's features. Noticing the creases and moles; the crooked shape of his nose all contribute to the accuracy.

What do I like about this piece?

How do I feel about the finished piece now? I'm pleased with it. The composition is good and there's a nice balance to the piece. You immediately notice the piercing eyes of the artist as he stare's intently at his model; trying to take in the minute details of his subjects form, to replicate with his brush and palette.

As an onlooker, you walk past this piece and notice the Artists look is fixed on you. It makes you a little anxious. No matter where in the room you go; his stare is on you. I hope you get that same feeling.

What I don't like.

Maybe I could have added a few darker tones to the furrows in his forehead and around the eyes to help balance the subject. If I'd learned from the example of the Ballerina, I could also darker the background more to really pull the onlookers focus to the eyes and face. Maybe I'll do that in the future; watch this space.

A Classic Western
Paul Newman – stage one

At the end of 2016 I challenged myself by attempting to draw two characters in one of my art pieces. This was particularly nerve racking as I'd only ever drawn one character in all of my portraits, needless to say; the drawing was a success and is proudly presented on my lounge wall.

Yes, you've probably guessed what the drawing was. It was the two cowboys Butch Cassidy and the Sundance Kid. I don't know what drew me to this piece but I love it, and so, it's not for sale.

I do have the image of the artwork on my Saatchi site at saatchiart.com/dragstar61 and many people have liked the piece to date. I know I drew this in December 2016 only two months after I took that journey into pointillism. I thought it would be an interesting exercise to reproduce the same portrait exactly twelve months later to see if those twelve months practice would make a difference.

You've just seen the initial drawing of Paul Newman. I've filled in the outline with small dots and added some of the darker area's to bring shape to the subject. I think I'll move on and start Robert Redford.

Robert Redford – stage one

The importance of drawing two characters on one page has definitely got to be the positioning of each character. I think I've succeeded in getting that right, so on with adding the basics down for Robert. As with Paul, I've drawn the outline and filled in with the smaller marker pen to build up some shape. I then added the darker marker pen to the very dark area's like the brim of his hat and under the flaps of his raincoat.

I think its time to add more shading to get to stage two.

Paul Newman – stage two

Here I've added more shading to the hat to bring a sense of texture and applied more shading to the face to show contours and shape. Finally I added some shading to the jacket. Time to do bring Roberts character up to stage two.

Robert – stage two

Added more filling in around the face to build up the shape, then, filled in the moustache. I added some darker shading to the hat and finally material lines for the jacket to complete stage two.

The Cowboys – Butch and Sundance

Completed December 2017 on Arches Velin Paper 200gsm 56cm x 76cm

The Cowboys

It's been exactly one year since I first draw Robert Redford and Paul Newman using pointillism. I wanted to see if I'd improved over that time by reproducing the same piece of art.

What do I like about this piece?

Comparing the two now; I can see that the detail has greatly improved. I'm glad that I took on this challenge as it's all too obvious that I had improved. Do I like this new piece? Yes. The composition is nicely set out and the balance is good with the two characters.

What I don't like.

It's interesting that although this piece has a lot more detail in, I still prefer the original piece I did last year. Maybe it's because the original leaves a lot more to your imagination. The original piece has more blank spaces that in a sense forces your mind to fill in. Don't get me wrong, I like this piece but I prefer the original.

Anne – stage one

Proportions laid out with particular attention to the eyes, nose and mouth. If I don't get those features correct from the start, she's not going to look like my wife. I think it's time to add some darker shading now.

Anne – stage two

What a relief to know that she's starting to look like the woman I married. Now the darker shading has pulled the subject together, I can start to add more layers and layers of finer shading to build up the contours and tones. Onto stage three.

Anne

Completed 3 December 2017 on Archers Velin paper 200gsm 56cm x 76cm

<u>Anne</u>

I dedicate this picture to my lovely wife whom I've been married to for thirty four years. This image was taken from a photograph of her when we first met

What do I like about this piece?

I'm pleased with the result considering the original photograph was taken with an old camera and the subject was largely in shadow. It's not a perfect representation of my wife, but it's close enough to recognise her.

What I don't like.

Again, because I was working from an old photograph that didn't show too much detail I'm not happy with not being able to show more detail to the hair and face. Would I attempt to work from an old photograph again? The answer would have to be NO. Having no other reference work to build an accurate piece of artwork, I feel I didn't do my wife enough justice.

Mary

Completed Dec 2017 on A2 cartridge paper

Mary

Mary Sato is an amateur photographer and model who follows me on my Instagram Page. Having seen the beautiful photographs she'd posted, I had to draw her.

I wanted to capture the strong contrast between dark and light with this piece so I decided to return to an earlier style of drawing that I'd used when drawing my Granddaughter Alexis. The strong dark contrast between the hair, facial features and shadow really work well with the dark bold black alongside the pale complexion.

What do I like about this piece?

I like the simplicity with this piece. The solid block of black for the hair with the individual light colour for the highlights builds shape and composition as it frames the subject. You're immediately drawn to Mary's beautiful captivating eyes as her gaze follows you around the room. You try to look away for a moment but then your eyes return to the subject.

What I don't like.

Maybe if I'm being critical, I would possibly darken the hair by filling in any gaps to make it a solid block. I would still leave the highlighted lines. I think the darker hair would definitely force your focus directly to Mary's pleading eyes.

Incomplete One

Completed Jan 2018 on A2 cartridge paper

Incomplete One

I decided to draw a series of 'Incomplete' portraits, this being the first in the series. So why have I decided not finished this piece?

Quite simply, I wanted to draw a portrait of a subject where the focus was on one section. In this case it is the girls face. The hand on the left of the piece combing back the hair is insignificant so I left the outline of the arm and hand so you can identify the body part.

The main focus is the woman's eyes as she looks back over her shoulder. What is she looking at? Has she just seen someone she likes and so combs back her hair so the other person can see the whole of her face? Maybe, or maybe it's something totally different.

I felt that the piece has the right amount of detail with the dark hair outline and strong eye makeup and lipstick to draw your focus. I felt the rest of the external detail was unimportant so I kept it our.

What do I like about this piece?

I like the eyes and lips framed by the dark hair.

What I don't like.

Maybe the face is a little too flat. Looking at it now, I can see I could have added more depth using the smaller dots to create contour and tone.

Incomplete Two

Completed January 2018 on A2 cartridge paper

Incomplete Two

Feeling pleased with my self from the last piece of artwork, I
decided to continue with the Incomplete series. This time I decided
to central the subjects eyes horizontally on the page to balance the
piece a little more.

Using the dark block of hair at the top right with the dark shading for
her shoulder presents the face off nicely.

What I like about this piece?

I added more detail to the hand because I felt it connected with the
subject and what I wanted to portray. I like also the increase of
darker shading around the facial features to balance the piece.

What I don't like.

I think I should have added a little more detail to the lady's right
arm. Maybe a darker outline to define the arm more, or just
something to the left of the arm to make clear what lies beyond what
is defined.

Hardy

Completed January 2018 on A2 cartridge paper

Hardy

This is a portrait of Tom Hardy in the film Taboo. Why did I draw Tom Hardy? The simple fact; I find him to be an extraordinary Actor worthy of recognition, and so felt compelled to draw him.

There were so many images of Tom I could have chosen from but decided on this one wearing a hat and fashioning a full beard. The light coming in from the left and slightly behind left a crescent of light reflecting along the length of his nose; with nothing behind the subject it looks like his nose is somewhat smaller than it is. I could have darkened the background so that his nose would be clearly seen, but felt the subject was mainly in shadow anyway and because he's wearing a large black hat. This could have taken the focus away from Tom's expression and stare.

What I like about this piece?

There's a lot of dark in this portrait, I particularly like the shading around the face and chin that clearly shows off his beard

What I don't like.

I would add more shading under the peak and rim of his hat to take away the overly dark pupil of his eye. Maybe I'll return to this piece sometime in the future and do just that. For now, I think I need to move on.

Maira

Completed February 2018 on A2 cartridge paper

<u>Maira</u>

Keeping with the same style from my previous pieces contrasting bold dark and light, I wanted to include an African female to my artwork.

What I like about this piece?

I liked the deep dark eyes with beautiful features.

What I don't like.

Looking back at this work, I think I could have darkened the hair to match the dark eye makeup and maybe added more shading to the face to get a clearer sense of her cheek bones.

Incomplete Three

Completed February 2018 on A2 cartridge paper

Incomplete Three

This piece following my incomplete series was a little different from my previous two in that the lady has blonde hair. Why is that of significance? Basically, the contrasting partnership between the bold black portions of hair with the pale skin couldn't be achieved with this piece.

So I had to change the focus, not from light and shade but to the beautiful pensive look of a pretty woman lost in her own thoughts.

I still used the dark bold shading to create the flow and body of her hair while the use of a smaller pen knib to create a more detailed composition of her facial features, really brings your focus to those eyes and thoughtful expression.

I purposely left the detail from the lady's hand as a detailed hand would have drawn your attention away from what I felt to be the most important. I hope you agree.

What I like about this piece?

I like it; it's different from the others while it has its own characteristics and appeal.

What I don't like.

I'm really in two minds as to whether I really like the blonde hair or should I have kept to the dark hair. It's different from the others but does it work? Yes, no. I'm still not sure. I'll let you decide.

Yusuf – Early stage of completion

After two days work the piece is starting to take shape. Having completed the initial stage using pencil, then filling in the outline with small dots and now the dark thick marker to fill in the beard, eyes and glasses, the overall look of the piece is coming together.

Yusuf

Completed February 2018 on A2 cartridge paper

Yusuf

Yusuf was quite interesting to draw in that I work with him. Looking at this completed piece, I think I've captured his character. The challenge for me was the glasses. Because Yusuf work thick lenses the image of his face decreased greatly. This had to be factored in when drawing the overall piece. It looks like were seeing background to the left of his right eye. This was the effect of his lenses. For accuracy, I had to include this within the piece.

What I like about this piece?

There's a good balance between dark shading and detail. The dark beard and dark shadows around his hair really frames his face. His head is perfectly positioned on the page and fills the page to an acceptable level.

What I don't like.

I don't dislike any of this work.

Drawing inside the lines – First in a series – nude one

Completed April 2018 on A2 sized cartridge paper.

Nude one

Using lines to define the subject can hold a piece together. In my previous portraits, the lines were created using dots; in fact the whole piece of artwork was created solely with the use of dots. Here I wanted to allow a few lines to outline my subject then complete the picture using pointillism.

Looking at the finished piece, the lines have tidied the piece together even when the pointillism dots fall outside the lines. It's interesting that from a distance, the smaller random dots outside the lines create a kind of haze; almost appearing as bodily heat rising from the subject. The lines outlining the body, definitely gives the subject a defined shape.

What I like about this piece?
The overall appearance is tidy and clean

What I don't like.
I initially wanted to keep the hair as an untouched space because my main focus was on the lined outline of the body. Now that I've finished the piece, I'm not so sure. I like the contrasting elements having the body complete and the hair unfinished but the more I look at it, the more I feel the need to fill in the hair. After a while I come back to this piece and like what I see. I think I'll just leave it as it is.

Life Drawing – Nude Two – Drawing inside the lines

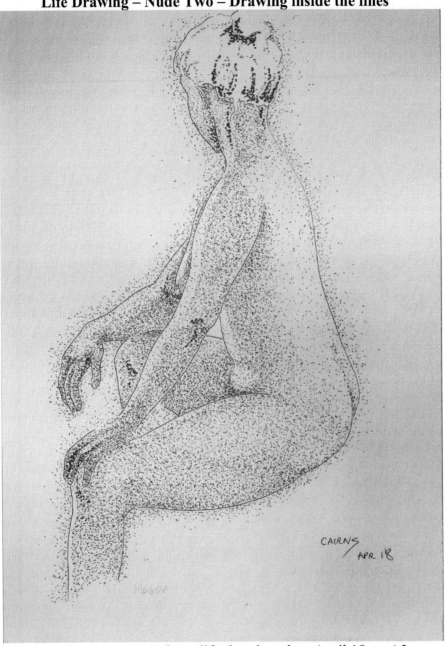

This piece was created at a life drawing class April 18 on A3
Cartridge Paper

Life Drawing – Nude two

I wanted to keep to the theme of drawing an outline, then filling the internal space with detail. Having enjoyed drawing inside the lines on an earlier piece, I thought I could try using the same technique at a Life Drawing Class.

This wasn't as easy as I'd originally thought; I hadn't factored in the problem with the time constraints usually applied to the life models. The model would hold her pose for fifteen minutes before changing position. Using pointillism as a means of putting an image down on paper would normally take around 8 – 10 hours of continuous work. I had fifteen minutes so I had to get down as much detail as possible and try to remember where the light sources came from for each pose, as I wouldn't be able to return to the piece for a few days.

What I like about this piece?
I definitely like the fact that I'd used an outline, it gave the subject shape.

What I don't like.
Not being able to return to this piece for several days was a problem. I had to remember exactly how the light reflected off the subject as well as remembering tone, contour and shade. If I had drawn the subject on a separate sheet using charcoal; the image would be clear. Unfortunately using pointillism to build up shade is such a lengthy process and having already waited over a week to get to this point, I feel the overall shading needs to be fuller, but I can't remember by how much.

Bronte – stage one

This is showing the first stage of completing on of my pieces. As you can see, I used the bolder, thicker knib marker pen to lay down the bold darker areas of the piece; this immediately adds shape to the piece.

Bronte – Finished

Completed April 2018 on A2 Cartridge Paper

Bronte

This was a good example showing bright light and shadow. The majority of the artwork is done with dark thick marker while the subtle detail around the lighter areas I used a fine knib marker.

Could I have continued and filled in more detail? Sure. But looking at it now, I think I stopped at the right time. I like it

On to my next drawing I think.

What I like about this piece?

I like the overall look of this piece. The sharp contrast between dark and light is very striking. The dark shading down the left side works well with the light on the right. The subject is nicely positioned and fills the page nicely.

What I don't like.

Maybe I could have added a small reflective glint in her eyes as I feel maybe they're a little too dark and so lacking in humanity.

Taking a bath

Completed Beginning of May 2018 on A2 Cartridge Paper

Taking a Bath

Going back to my usual style of creating the subject just using dots, you can see the distinct difference. There are no bold lines to break up the flow of natural anatomical structure. The body becomes one. There are no separation between hair, face, head and torso.

Using the smaller dots to create tone and contour really comes to the fore; this technique does however require the input of lots and lots and lots of dots. In contrast, the use of a darker thicker knib lends to a distinct separation from one part to another. It's fine and acceptable when areas need to stand out, as in the case of the subject's dark hair and deeper shadow but again, this needs to be limited in use and not overwhelm the overall piece.

What I like about this piece?

The subject is positioned well and the balance of the piece is nice. The detail is good around the skin tones and it has a nice feel.

What I don't like.

Maybe I could have added more detail to show the walls of the bathtub that the woman is sat in to lend to the story. But overall, I'm pleased with the piece as a whole.

Muse

Completed May 2018 on A2 Cartridge Paper

Muse

Here I've reverted back to completely using dots to outline my subject. This piece was completed on an A2 sheet of cartridge paper at the beginning of May 2018.

What I like about this piece?

The overall subject is nicely positioned to fill the page to a satisfactory level. I like the detail which comes through nicely displaying tone and contour. The hair, with its highlights conveys shape and wave. I feel the overall piece is nicely balanced with the darker hair lending to the dark shadow running diagonal south west to the subjects hips.

What I don't like.

I could have added a little more detail especially around the back of the knee and maybe the hamstrings but apart from that, I'm happy with the overall look of this piece.

Muse Two

Completed May 2018 on A2 Cartridge Paper

Muse Two

I love this piece, it's sexy and it's fun. The blonde is grinning maybe at her husband bringing her breakfast in bed and he's holding a tray, standing completely naked?

I used the smaller knib pen to create the fleshly tones; adding layer upon layer until I could show contour and tone. The darker area's around the face, hair folds and deep crevice between her bicep and bust give the piece enough detail and shape.

I added just enough shading in the bed sheet to show the fold and creases in the material as she clutches the material to her chest to maintain an air of decency.

What I like about this piece?

The overall composition is nice and central to the paper. I like that there's not one area that draws your attention. The blonde hair with the darker shadows are not overbearing and blends nicely with the tones around the body.

What I don't like.

There isn't anything specifically that I don't like about this piece. Maybe at some future time, I may look back and think 'that's not right! Or 'I don't like that' but until that time comes. I'm happy.

Muse in the dark

Completed May 2018 on A2 Cartridge Paper

Muse in the Dark

I like the dark contrast between light and shadow which is clearly seen in this piece of art. The light source comes from opposite sides reflecting the front and rear of the subject outlining shape clearly. Positioning the subject in a dark room with two spotlights shining from opposite sides allows the artist to focus on the shading more so than the light; a total reversal of what is normal.

What I like about this piece?

I like the fact that it's the reflective areas of the subject that are visible. The dark borders forces your focus on the light and from what we can just make out; we form the shape of a female on her knees. It's a simple concept and quite effective.

What I don't like.

I don't have any reservations about this piece. Overall I'm happy with it.

Twisted Nude

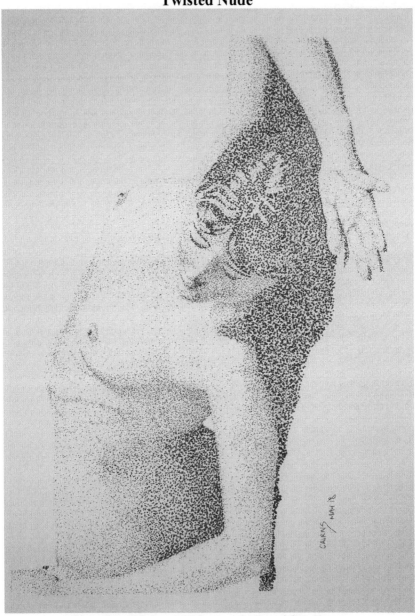

Completed May 2018 on A2 Cartridge Paper

<u>Twisted Nude</u>

Using the strong contrast between light and shade, I wanted to have a large dark area of my artwork to immediately draw the onlooker's eyes towards. Not clearly identifiable, this dark object may appear for a moment as abstract; but then you take in the rest of the piece and you recognise the subject. Lying on the bed with her left knee raised and her back arched and twisted gave me the title of this piece.

What I like about this piece?

I like the dark hair running parallel to the dark shadow running across the page. The piece feels balanced and well presented. The twist in the torso adds depth to the overall piece.

What I don't like.

I could have added a little more depth from the dark shadow to the reflective light but otherwise I'm pleased with this piece.

Muse Four

Completed this drawing on the last day in May 2018

Muse Four

Looking slightly up at my subject with the light source high and to the right gave me another viewpoint using light and shade. Having my subject stand in a darkened room with the single light source highlighting a fraction of her body allowed me to use the thicker marker pen for the dark areas and the thinner marker for the detail.

What I like about this piece?

I like the limited reflective areas of the woman's torso to immerse from the darkness. The simplicity of the piece is quite refreshing. There's enough detail in the light area to identify who the subject is without having to reveal any more.

What I don't like.

I could have built up the detail around the face a little better. The hairline could have been softer; showing more of the face. It looks too boxy for my liking.

Muse Five

Completed June 2018 on A3 Cartridge Paper

Muse Five

I purposely used just the fine marker pen to create this piece. I wanted to keep the overall flow of the piece; and this could be achieved using the same size dots. Had I used a larger marker to define the darker shades would have created too much of a contrast.

I'm quite pleased with the end result. The models muscular definition is nicely portrayed showing tone and contour.

What I like about this piece?

The subject is positioned nicely and central to the page. I like the definition and detail of the muscles particularly in her left arm.

What I don't like.

The shading around the face could have been better to show depth. There's some detail missing from her chest, maybe from strands of hair hanging down.

Buttocks

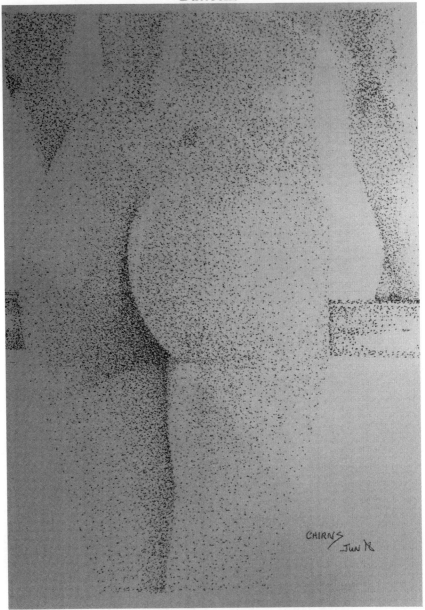

Completed June 2018 on A3 cartridge paper

Buttocks

This was a tough one to complete; the subject not only had light and shade but contour and tone. Why do I say that, surely all subjects have those? As explained before, drawing skin tones using dots to create shape and shadow can be difficult in itself; with this subject, we have strong light coming from two directions which can almost obliterate the shape of the subject. Trying to draw light reflective areas as well as trying to show shape can be a conflicting battle. Too much light and the detail is gone; too much detail and the light reflective areas are gone.

What I like about this piece?

The overall piece is nicely positioned. The subject fills the page and the details are sufficient to allow the onlookers to recognise the image. I like the reflective areas. They give contrast and shape to the subject.

What I don't like.

There's always going to be a battle between deciding how far to take a piece. Do I add more detail or should I finish? I could have added and added more and more detail; but to be honest, I'm happy with what I had achieved. I like the look of this piece and in the future if I decide to add more detail, I'm sure it will look even better. For now, I'm happy.

Stockings

I completed this portrait on A2 sized cartridge paper 9th June 2018.

Stockings

I focussed more on the skin tones as opposed to the hair so there was more detail on the body to show contour and shape. I enjoyed drawing this subject and felt that I could have continued adding more and more depth to the skin tones. Maybe it's something I would go back to at a later date. For now I think I'll move on to my next project.

What I like about this piece?

It has a nice feel. The subject is nicely positioned. The detail I'm happy with and the composition is good.

What I don't like.

Maybe I could have added a little more detail; maybe a little darker shadow under her thigh. Else I'm happy with this piece.

Shower

Completed this piece on the 10th June 2018.

Shower

Having spent hours trying to get the shading right. I enjoyed doing this subject because it gave me an added challenge in creating the water droplets. I had drawn a female taking a shower last year but didn't include the water. Looking at this completed piece, I'm glad I did add the water and I'm pleased with the end result.

What I like about this piece?

I think I added just the right amount of detail. I really get the sense of shape and contour so I'm happy.

What I don't like.

If I was to be overly critical, I could have added more droplets and maybe some running down her torso. Maybe in a future project

Silhouette

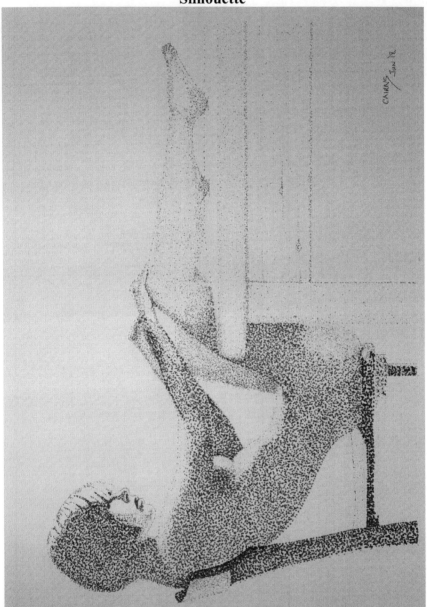

Completed 16th June 2018 on A2 Cartridge Paper

<u>Silhouette</u>

I really like this piece. It's simple but effective in capturing the story and mood of the subject. A light from the kitchen window shines in from the right, illuminating the female from her feet to her head.

What I like about this piece?

You would think having the light source from the right would create an imbalance with this piece, but no. The image tells a story. I like the simplicity. The overall composition is nice.

What I don't like.

Nothing.

Pregnant

Completed 18th June 2018 on A2 Cartridge Paper

Pregnant

What haven't I done with drawing nudes? A pregnant woman adds a certain special appeal; not only a beautiful woman, but one with baby. Again using the space available, I wanted to capture as much detail as possible. Bringing the subject close and concentrating on the most important aspect of this piece; being the stage of her pregnancy, I wanted to portray the love she has for her child. You can just imagine her looking down as her baby kicks out. The slight movement of skin around her protruding belly; reassures her that her child is safe and alive. You can just sense the love she has for her baby.

What I like about this piece?

The light from low and to the right highlights her body leaving the top of her head in shadow. I like the detail emphasising the pregnant woman. The stretched skin across her tummy; clearly showing the advanced stage of pregnancy she's in. The hands clutching her enlarged breasts; a further sign that she's pregnant.

What I don't like.

I could have added darker shading under the armpits and around the base of her breasts to show consistency with the darker shading under her chin and the top of her head. No doubt it's something I could go back and finish at a later date.

Hands on

Completed 4th July 2018 on A2 cartridge paper

Hands on

I completed the bulk of this piece using the small marker pen because I wanted to show as much detail as possible over the body surface. Using the finer dots afford you greater freedom in producing subtle tones that a larger marker could not.

The high sun shining straight down not only created shade but also shadow as can be seen by the shadow of the woman's head directly below her chin across the top part of her chest.

What I like about this piece?
The composition is nice as the subject is central and nicely positioned on the page. The smaller dots are quite effective in producing shape, shadow, tone and contour which I like. Overall, I'm happy with the finished piece.

What I don't like.
Looking back at the artwork now, I can see that maybe I shouldn't have put in reflective highlights on the lower part of her hair; particularly as the sun is right above.

Side Profile

Completed 7th July 2018 on A2 Cartridge Paper

Side Profile

Knowing how effective it was to use primarily the smaller marker pen, I decided to continue with this next piece in the same vein. The piece took me longer to complete but looking back now, I know I chose the right approach. The smaller dots certainly give you more detail.

What I like about this piece?

I like the composition, it feels nice. The subject fills the page to a satisfactory level. The dark hair immediately draws your attention but then allows you to glance down at her striking facial makeup and then to her well presented physical form.

What I don't like.

If I was to be overly critical at this point, maybe I would have added a little more body to her hair. Maybe also a few darker shadows under her armpit and around her right breast to balance the overall piece.

Luscious

Completed on A2 cartridge paper on 11th July 2018

Luscious

Why did I draw this piece of art? Having drawn full and half figures for the majority of my portraits, I thought it was time to bring in the subject to capture a bit more of the subjects personality. I named this piece 'Luscious' because of the sultry look she is giving. Is it a nude? Well again, the revealing of the woman's well formed left breast in the bottom left corner would confirm that she is a nude.

What I like about this piece?

I like the stark contrast between bold dark shadow and paler dark features. The dark borders competing with the detailed lighter features seem to battle for position. Your eyes are drawn to the dark edges because the darker areas take president over the detailed paler and more important area's outlining the beautiful face with her alluring look.

What I don't like.

At this point in time, I don't really dislike anything about this piece. My initial idea was to complete the portrait fully but having reached this stage, I decided to stop. I know there are sections which haven't been touched and there are sections which have some detail but not complete. The simple answer is I don't care. I like it as it is and to my mind it's finished.

I hope you like it too.

Conclusion

I've enjoyed putting together this book and showing you how I go about creating my artwork. Sometimes it's been a little nerve racking at times, not knowing how a piece would come together. In the end though, I've enjoyed it.

I want to take this opportunity in thanking you for purchasing this book.

I hope you've enjoyed reading my thoughts and opinions regarding the art pieces I'd completed over the past year. My wish is that you can feel inspired to have a go yourself and maybe in doing so, turn out fine art work for others to admire.

For me, I'm going to continue with pointillism because I like creating pieces of art just from dots.

Original Artwork and Prints available from:
Saatchiart.com/dragstar61

Kind Regards

Chris Cairns
Artist/Author